ubu royale

for James, as ever

ubu royale

Being M. Alfred Jarry's play "UBU ROI"
First produced in Paris, 1896
Englisshed ici par M. Neil Bartlett

First published in Great Britain in 2024 by
CHEERIO Publishing
www.cheeriopublishing.com
info@cheeriopublishing.com

Design: Mark and Keith at Mini Moderns®
Cover design: Tiana-Jane Dunlop
Cover photograph: *Still of Anthony Reynolds as Papa Ubu in the film Roi*
Photography by Jack Sadler. CHEERIO, 2023.

The moral right of the author has been asserted.

Any application for performance should be made before commencement of rehearsals to The Agency (London) Ltd, 24 Pottery Lane, Holland Park, London W11 4L2, or via email: info@theagency.co.uk. No performances may be given unless a licence has been obtained and no alterations may be made in the title or the text of the play without its authors written consent.

A CIP catalogue record for this book is available from the British Library.

ISBN: 9781739440510

some notes for the reader

LOTS OF THIS SO-CALLED 'PLAY' IS JUST BODILY
INCIDENT AND FUNCTION – BATTLES, PUNCH-UPS,
EXPLOSIONS, DOMESTICS, EATING, SHITTING, ETC.,
SO BE PREPARED TO READ BETWEEN THE ACTUAL
LINES FOR PHYSICAL BUSINESS OF THAT ILK.

IT IS ALSO WORTH REMEMBERING THAT THIS WAS
ORIGINALLY WRITTEN AS A PUPPET-SHOW,
SO THINGS HAPPEN WITH BODIES THAT WOULD NOT
BE LIKE REMOTELY ACCEPTABLE IN (I HESITATE
TO TYPE THE PHRASE) REAL LIFE.

ALSO, AS YOU WILL SEE, IN THIS RENDITION,
MÈRE AND PÈRE UBU DO THE POLICE IN
DIFFERENT VOICES. SOMETIMES THEY TALK LIKE THEY
IS DOING GRANT AND SHARON OFF
OLD TAPES OF EASTENDERS; SOMETIMES THEY TALK
POTTYMOUTH LIKE IN THAT ADMIRABLE FILM SEXY
BEAST. SOMETIMES PÈRE UBU TALKS LIKE CRIMINAL
DONALD – OR LIKE MINIDONALD, AKA DISGRACED
FORMER UK PRIME MINISTER CRIMINAL BORIS.
SOMETIMES THEY DO THE ACTUAL SHAKESPEARE.
WHATEVER. GO WITH IT.
CONSISTENCY IS FOR LOSERS.

dramatis personae

Père Ubu
Mère Ubu

and;

In Poland;
Good King Wenceslarse
Fair Queen Rosamonder
Their three sons; Crown Prince Buggerlarse,
Prince Taggerlarse and Prince Ruggerlarse
Ubu's fellow Captain of the Royal Bodyguard,
Captain Crappering
The Royal Bodyguards – aka The Lads Army

The Ghost of Matthias 1st of Konisberg
A Load of Other Ghosts
The voice of Sigismond The Unready
A Few Royal Serving Drudges
The People of Poland, inc Mikhael Fedorovitch
Posh People
Bankers, Judges, Solicitors
Peasants, inc. Stanislarse Leczinski (an old peasant)
Royal cash-grabbers who work for Ubu once he is King
Gaolers at Ubu's Castle Dunce-inane
Amongst Ubu's rebel-rabble; Private Prompt,
Corporal Cordon, Lt Nickelarse Nackleby
General Flunk, Lieutenant Musclefuck

In Russia;
Tsar Alexis
His Court
His Army

In A Cave In The Ukraine
Corporal Crashbang and Private Wallop
(Ubu's Last Camp-Followers Once He Has Been Defeated In
The War)
An Echo
A Ginormous Bear

On A Boat
A Captain

**The play takes place... In Poland, that is to say,
Nowhere.* Also Russia, Ukraine, Estonia, Engerland.**

* on account of when this play first occurred there was no such country
as Poland.

actonesceneone

Père Ubu   Ssssshate!!!

Mère Ubu   Langwidge, DaddyU!! You is always using words...

Père Ubu   And you, Mummy – *you* is cruisin' for a brusin'...

Mère Ubu   'Snot me you wannabe assassinating, DaddyU, 'tis someone else entirely.

Père Ubu   JesusHShiteShover, Mrs U., wot is you onnabout?

Mère Ubu   Why Daddy, surely you is not 'appy with this 'ere our current 'umble station in laife...?

Père Ubu   SteaminHTurdpiles, Mother – 'coarse I'm fuckin' 'appy. Look at me; Captain of the Guards – Knight Royal of the Chamberbed of His Royal Madge Good King Wenceslarse of Poloneyland – Knighteynight of the Order of the Big Red Royal Eaglebird Second Class – not to mention yer actual recently crownèd Prince of Fuckin' Aragon. I mean, whaddyafuckin'want, Mummy?

Mère Ubu   Yeah but yeah but yeah but Sure, Aragon's mean crownlet now thou hast – But content ye, sire, with such a lowly state? Bare fifty knights in tow – nay, fifty wankers – When – but one royal death... what's this I see? – Fair Poland's crown encircling then thy bonce...

Père Ubu   Come again?

1

Mère Ubu	Fuck me you is thick sometimes, Daddy.
Père Ubu	DrippinH. Arsepiles, Mummy – Our King Good Wencelarse reigns yet – and deaded if he was, has't not royal kiddies aplenty?
Mère Ubu	Yeah but so you dead them also. Simples.
Père Ubu	Mummy, you is doin' my head in – and sure forsooth, in severe imminence of a stretch in pokey thou currently art'st, what with this 'ere treasonous royal deading chit-chat.
Mère Ubu	Well you'd better watch out then Daddy, 'cause if I ends up in poke, who's gonna mend them splits you gets in yer trousers. Eh?
Père Ubu	Fuck off you in pokeypoke. No way. Besides, my arse looks good hanging out a bit.
Mère Ubu	Your arse deserves a *throne*, Daddy. Come on... Think of the money. Think of all the sausages. Think of you an me drivin' down our road in a fuckin' *carriage*...
Père Ubu	Yeah but yeah but yeah but YEAH – if I was King, I could 'ave a crown, like what the one I got from the Aragon jobbie before those Spanish bastards nicked it. But like... bigger.
Mère Ubu	And one of those whatsit umbrolly things. And a cloak, what comes down to your toes...
Père Ubu	Oh fuck I'm givin' way now Mrs U... Yeah! Shit on my dick and say thank you, Wenceslarse – he meets me down a dark alleyway anytime soon, he's gonna be sorry...

Mère Ubu	Oh DaddyU, once you gets the idea, you is the total Bollocks.
Père Ubu	Wadeaminnit!!! Me – Captain of 'is very own Guard – kill our very own King of Poloneyland? I could get deaded myself!
Mère Ubu	*[ASIDE.]* Sssshate! *[ALOUD.]* O, right, yeah, be my guest – live like fuckin' churchmice foreeverandever why don't we!
Père Ubu	Shiting H. Shitefuck, Mrs.! – rather a poor honest fuckmouse than a dead bent fatcat. Right?
Mère Ubu	So no crownhatting for Daddy?? No cloakytoes? No umbrolly...?
	[PÈRE UBU THINKS ABOUT IT, AND IS TORN – BUT HIS COWARDICE GETS THE BETTER OF HIM.]
Père Ubu	Nah. Shove it right up there, Mother!
	[EXITS, SLAMMING DOOR.]
Mère Ubu	*[BURPS.]* Shate. Well, scene one, innit – any plot's bound to be a *bit* slippy to start with. *[BURPS.]* Still, think I got 'im a bit stiff for it... Thank you, O Lord – no thank *you*, Mummy – and watch this space. Eight days from now, I'm gonna be Queen of fuckin' Poland.

actonescenetwo

a room chez ubu, one featuring a splendidly laid table.

Mère Ubu	They is late.
Père Ubu	Turdsontoastforbreakfast they is late – and I'm fuckin' starvin'. May I say, Mother, how specially rank you're lookin today. I presumes that's on behalf of how we is expectin guests?
Mère Ubu	*[SHRUGGING.]* Fuck'em.
Père Ubu	Fuckem it is. I could eat the arse off that chicken.
	[HE EATS THE ARSE OFF A CHICKEN...]
	Hmmnnn. 'Snot bad.
Mère Ubu	Getcherandsoff! What are my guests going to fuckineat, eh?
Père Ubu	There's plenny to go round! Alright alright, I wont fuckin' touch it. Tell you what... why don't you stick your 'ead out the winder and see if they're coming, Mother.
	[SHE DOES.]
Mère Ubu	Can't see nuffin...
	[PÈRE UBU TAKES THIS OPPORTUNITY TO HELP HISSELF TO A SLICE OF VEAL.]
	Oh no, there's Captain Crappering and his Lad's Army coming up pronto. And what the fuck is you gobblin now, Daddy?
Père Ubu	Nuffin. Sliceoveal.

4

Mère Ubu	*[ADAPTING RICHARD 3ᴿᴰ.]* The veal – the veal – he eats the fuckin' veal. Give me Strength!
Père Ubu	JesusHSloppyfuck, I am so gonna punch your fuckin' lights out innerminnit –
	[THEY SCRAP. THE DOOR OPENS, IN COMES CAPTAIN CRAPPERING AND HIS BRIGADE.]

actonescenethree

Mère Ubu	Gentlemen! – we was wondering when you'd get here, praydobeseated...
Capt. Crap	Good day madam lady. But where forsooth is Our Father which art the Ooboo?
	[PÈRE HAD ENDED UP UNDER THE TABLE AND NOW HOISTS HIMSELF WITH DIFFICULTY (ON ACCOUNT OF HIS GIRTH) INTO A CHAIR.]
Père Ubu	Here I am here I am... bugger me shitless I'm puttin' it on.
Capt. Crap	And good-day to you, DaddyU. Platoon, At Ease!
	[EVERYBODY SITS AT TABLE.]
Père Ubu	Give us a mo, this fuckin' chair's too small...
	[HE GETS HIMSELF SORTED.]
Capt. Crap	So Madame Ooboo, what treats hast thou in store for us this day?
Mère Ubu	And today's specials are –
Père Ubu	Oh yeah! I always like it when they do this bit...

Mère Ubu	For starters, Soupe à la Polognaise; then, chops à la posh; pâté à la Alsatian; Roast Turd-key; Charlotte Arse –
Père Ubu	Fuckinell, push the fuckin' boat out why don't you –
Mère Ubu	Bumbe surprise; Jerusalem Fartichokes; Cauliflower Oh Shat-in; coffee liquers'n chocolates to follow –
Père Ubu	Oi, whooze payin for all this, Richard Fuckin' Branson?
Mère Ubu	Oh please don't maiind my 'usband gentlemen, 'e can be such a thickperson sometames.
Père Ubu	You, is going to feel my fistyfist right up your inside leg measurement in just a minute –
Mère Ubu	Now do eat up, Daddy, here's a nice spot of hot poloney what I done for you special –
Père Ubu	Fuck me, that's rank –
Capt. Crap	Well yes, it is *slightly* nasty akcherly –
Mère Ubu	Expecting Halal, were you? Kosher? Veggicuntingtarian?!?
	[PÈRE UBU SLAPS HIS FOREHEAD.]
Père Ubu	'Scuse me – just had an idea... back in a mo.
	[EXIT PÈRE UBU.]
Mère Ubu	Gentlemen can I interest you in a spot of veal meanwhile?
Capt. Crap	Oh very nice. All gone.
Mère Ubu	A slice of Turdkey?
Capt. Crap	Oh delicious. Let's hear it for Mamma Ooboo!!

Craps Army	Mamma Ooh-ooh-ooh-ooh, Boo-hoo-hoo hoo *etc etc*...!
	[PÈRE UBU RETURNS WITH AN UNMENTIONABLE SPECIES OF BRUSH AND FLICKS FAECAL MATTER AT HIS GUESTS.]
Père Ubu	And now let's hear it for DaddyOoboo! DADDYOO-OO-OO-OO *etc*!!
Mère Ubu	Oh you filthy beast, what is you doing?
Père Ubu	Go on, give it a lick!
	[SEVERAL GUESTS TASTE A BIT AND IMMEDIATELY SUCCUMB TO FOOD-POISONING.]
Père Ubu	Mummy, might you pass the choplets? I'll do the honours.
Mère Ubu	Cummin' right up...
Père Ubu	Right ladz; everybody out!!
Craps Lads	What about our dinner?
Père Ubu	Yervadyereffingdinnernoweffofftheloddervya!! Not you, Crappering – a word.
	[NOBODY MOVES.]
	CrappingHCrapfuck; last one out gets a cutlet up the shitter!!
	[HE STARTS TO LOB CUTLETS.]
Army Lads	Oooh! Aaaargh! Help! Oopsy-daisy!!!!
Père Ubu	EffoffEFFOFFEFFOFF!! That's the way to do it!!!
The Lads	Run for it, lads!! That Daddy's a BadDaddy!! 'Eez a Cheapshate! Eez a TrumpsterDumbster!!!!

Père Ubu	Well thank goodness they've gone. Do excuse me while I catch my breath – and I say, that's quite fucked the entire dining experience, what? Come, Crappering, let us retire...

[THE THREESOME EXIT.]

actonescenefour

a neighbouring room.

Père Ubu	So, how was dinner for you, Captain?
Capt. Crap	Personly, I could've done without the shit.
Père Ubu	Personly, I thought it was quite a good one...
Mère Ubu	Shackern arson gute.
Père Ubu	Captain Crappering... what thinkst thou of bein' Duke of Lithuania...?
Capt. Crap	Lies that in thy power, Daddy?
Père Ubu	Give it a few days... and yew is lookin at yer new actual King.
Capt. Crap	You don't mean... you don't mean you is planning to dead Wenceslarse!
Père Ubu	Top marks for this one, not such a daft bugger as he looks...
Capt. Crap	Count me in, Daddy – I 'ate that there GKW. And you may count my loyal ladz in also.
	[PÈRE UBU THROWS HIMSELF ON THE CAPTAIN TO EMBRACE HIM.]
Père Ubu	I fucking love you –
Capt. Crap	Whoa! Daddy! You don't wash yer 'ands after, do ya?

8

Père Ubu	Not often.
Mère Ubu	Not never.
Père Ubu	Someone round ere's going to get fuckin' kneecapped in a minute –
Mère Ubu	Shatester!
Père Ubu	Right, Captain, that's yer lot for now. But by ShitingHshitecrap I swear – on my fuckin' wife's life, when I am King, Duke of Lithuania thou shalt be soonest.
Mère Ubu	What the –
Père Ubu	Shuttit, sweetlips.
	[OFF CRAPPERING GOES.]
	[AND SO, DEAR READER, PÈRE UBU'S ASCENT TO POWER IS BEGUN...]

actonescenefive

	[A MESSENGER ENTERS.]
Père Ubu	Watchoowand? Buggerroffowdervit – you doughnarfmakemetired.
Messenger	Sire, you are summoned by the King, forthwith.
	[THE MESSENGER LEAVES.]
Père Ubu	Shate! Shatingshate-shatefuck!! Hairy Mary!!! I am discovered. 'Tis the chopper for me, Mother.
Mère Ubu	What a fuckin' wimp. I must screw his courage to the shitting place –
Père Ubu	Wadeaminnit; I got an idea. I'll say it was all you and Crappering what done it –

9

Mère Ubu	You nasty fat piece of... listen, D.U.; you say it was us, and I'll –
Père Ubu	Watch me.
	[HE LEAVES.]
Mère Ubu	Daddy! Daddy Ooboo!! Come back! I'll do you a nice fresh hot sausage...
	[SHE GOES AFTER HIM.]
Père Ubu	*[STICKING HIS HEAD OUT THE WINGS.]* Shite me sideways, all that woman ever thinks about is where the next hot sausage is coming from...

actonescenesix

the palace of king wenceslarse, surrounded by his guards, captain crappering, and the king's three sons; buggerlarse, taggerlarse and ruggerlarse. later, père ubu.

Père Ubu	Listen, mate, honest – it was Mummy U and that Captain Crappering wot done it.
The King	Come again, Daddy U?
Capt. Crap	He's pissed, your madge.
The King	Only like what we was this morning...
Père Ubu	'Tis truth, Sir, that I art somewhat wazzed... but only from drinking thy' ealth... Honest.
The King	Daddy Oob, notwithstanding thy pissedness, we are minded to reward you for your many valiances as captain of our royal guard, and so intend to make you Count of Sandomierz.* * (a regional capital of Eastern Poland, now a major tourist and cultural centre, and also an important centre of historic anti-Semitism – translator's note)

Père Ubu   Oh Sire, I don't know how to thank you enough I'm sure.

The King   Never mind thanking me, just turn up on time for the investiture.

Père Ubu   I'm there, Boss. Meanwhile, pray accept this mine humble kazoo, as a token of my loyalty.

The King   Do I look like I still fuckin' play with my kazoo? Yon young Crown Prince Buggerlarse shall take it up.

Buggerlarse   Kazoo wazoo! Thou hast a fuckin' laugh, Ubu.

Père Ubu   HahahahahHA!! And now, my liege, I shall fuck off. *[HE TURNS TO GO AND FALLS OVER.]* Aaah!! OooooaaawwShittingHshirtlifters – I've only gone and shivered my spleen and puckered my pucking poopcrack...

The King   *[HELPING HIM UP.]* What, Father Ubu – art'st thou injurèd?

Père Ubu   Cruelly, Sire, and like to die. Mother Ubu – what shall become of her?

The King   We shall take good care of her, never fear.

Père Ubu   You've a good 'art, Sire, for sure *[ASIDE, EXITING.]* But look thee, O Wenceslarse – fair heart 'ne're stayed th'assassin's hand!!!

actonesceneseven

chez ubu encore.

mère, père, crappering, the lads.

Père Ubu	Friends, Romans, Cunts – right – what we need, is a plan. Now, I want everyone to chip in, but I'll go first –
Capt. Crap	Silence please for Daddy.
Père Ubu	OK. Friends, I reckon... we poison 'im... by sticking arse-nic up his lunchbox. He schloomfs a royal sandwich – he kicks the royal bucket – Long Live Ubu King. Yeah?
Omnes	Nah. Bollocks.
Père Ubu	What? Whassyaproblem? Alright – Crappering, let's hear your angle.
Capt. Crap	I reckon... single sword-thrust – right in the nickerknacks. That's the way to do it.
Omnes	Hear, hear! They don't call him Captain Crappster for nothing!!
Père Ubu	Yeah but, yeah but – what if he kicks you up the arse? On investiture days, right, Wenceslarse wears these metal boots, which can really do some damage. Oh yeah. And anyway, now you've told me the plan, I'm going to grass up the lot of you, that way I'd be in the clear, right, totally – and he'll probably give me a reward too!!!
Mère Ubu	Oh you nasty big piece of treacherous lardarse!!!
Omnes	Shame! Shame!!!

Père Ubu   Oi! Gents! Pipe down, or some of you are
deffo going to get dropped right in it, OK?
Alright, for your sake, lads, I'll risk it;
Plan B; slice'n'dice.

Capt. Crap   OK yeah... but maybe it would be like,
better, yeah, if we all just jumped on top of
him all at the same time, all sort of like all
shouting and yelling, yeah? That way we
could sort of maybe nobble all his soldiers
as well yah?

Père Ubu   OK, yeah; great – great – I tread on his toes
– accidentally on purpose; he kicks me; I
shout SHITESTER!!! – that's the signal for
you all to jump him –

Mère Ubu   And soon as he's dead, I nab the
crown jewels.

Capt. Crap   And I head off toot sweet to hunt down
the rest of the royal family with the ladz
here – right?

Père Ubu   Yeah – and give that Crown Prince
CrackInYerArse one specially from
me, right?

*[EVERYONE EXITS, AND THEN
PÈRE UBU RUNS AFTER THEM AND
DRAGS THEM BACK.]*

Oioioioioi – angonerminnit, we forgot to do
the bit where we all swear. All for one
and one for me. Amen.

Capt. Crap   Yeah right – but for swearing, I mean you
need a vicar, right?

Père Ubu   Mummy U can do it. She often takes an
oaf.

Omnes Right! Yeah! Let's do it!!

Père Ubu OK; everybody; We do solemnly swear... to dead the king... but like *totally* dead, yeah, honest?

[MÈRE UBU TAKES THEIR SACRED OATH OF ALLEGIANCE.]

Omnes Yeah! Long Live The Oooboo!! Ooh-ooh-ooh-ooh; boo-hoo-hoo!! etc.

[HERE ENDETH THE FIRST ACT, WATCH OUT, WENCESLARSE!!!!]

acttwosceneone

the palais royale of poloneyland.

the royal family; king wenceslarse, queen rosamonder wenceslarse, crown prince buggerlarse, captain of the royal bodyguard (captain crappering), royal guards.

King W	Captain Crappering, you was most rude yesterday to Daddy Ooboo, our new-mint Cunt of Sandowierz. Thou and thy guards art banned therefore from attending this morning's Grand Parade.
Queen W	But Wenceslarse chéri, surely the *hole* royle fam'ly need not attend to protect you therefore?
King W	Madam, I have issued an executive instruction. You wear me out sometimes with this whinging you really fuckin' do.
Bugger	Sire, sire, see; *I* submit most loyally.
Queen W	But, Royale-ness most high, dost think it truly wise, to proceed un-guarded?
King W	Why not?
Queen W	Madgehusband, forgetst thou thus my last night's dolorous dream? I saw you lost beneath a bloody mass of arms, dumped in the River Fistula – while yea forsooth the red, red eaglebird of Poloneyland didst lower the circletroyal onto THAT ignoble-head.
King W	Whose 'ead?
Queen W	Why DaddyOoboozes. Sire.

15

King W	Pish! Pishpishposh! DaddyOoboo is most loyal – he'd let wild horses drag him through shit if I arsked him.
Queen W	O, dire misjudgement!
	[BUGGERLARSE GOES TO SPEAK IN HER SUPPORT.]
King W	Shut it, bastardfeatures.
	And as for you, Madame, let me show you just how much scaredy-scared I am; I shall now attend the Big Parade unarmed; no fuckin' shooter, no fuckin' blade.
Queen W	O, casualness fatale – sure, nevermore shallst I see thee living!!!
King W	Oi, Taggerlarse – Ruggerlarse – with me!
	[THEY EXIT. THE QUEEN AND PRINCE BUGGERLARSE GO TO THE WINDOW.]
Queen W	God and Holy Saint Nicklarse watch over thee, my husband!! Buggerlarse, follow me to the chapel and help me pray for your father and your royal brothers.
	[THEY GO.]

acttwoscenetwo

the royal parade ground.

king wenceslarse and princes taggerlarse and ruggerlarse inspect the troops. père ubu is in regalia of a cunt of sandomierz.

King W	Cunt Ubupop, kindly fall in the men for this inspection of the troops.
Père Ubu	*[ASIDE.]* OK, standby, you lot... just coming, your Madgesty, just coming...

King W	Ah, the First Danzig Mounted Cavalry. Splendid sight.
Père Ubu	You reckon? I think they're a complete fuckin'disgrace!! *[TO A CAVALRYMAN.]* Oi, fuckface, when did you last have a fuckin' shave???
King W	But this private presents totally pukka, forsooth. What's eating you, Ubupop?
Père Ubu	You are!!! *[STAMPING ON HIS TOE.]*
King W	Oh you beast!
Père Ubu	SHAAAAATSTAAH!! Get 'im, lads!!
Capt. Crap	Yowsa. Have at thee!!
	[EVERYONE JUMPS THE KING. EXPLOSION.]
King W	Oh! I die, I die! Holy Mary, pray for me now, and at the hour of my aaaaargh!
Taggerlarse	*[TO RUGGERLARSE.]* What noise is this! Brother, draw thy sword!
Père Ubu	Goddit – goddit – got the crown!! Right – now let's get the rest of 'em –
Capt. Crap	Get them traitors deaded!!!!
	[THE KING'S TWO SONS LEG IT, WITH EVERYBODY AFTER THEM.]

the chapelle royale.

queenie rosamonder and crown prince buggerlarse, just finishin' praying to god for protection for king wenceslarse.

Queen W	Well, that's a load off my mind I must say.
Bugger	You have nothing to fear.
	[A TERRIBLE UPROAR IS HEARD COMING FROM OUTSIDE.]
	Alas what's this I see? My two royal brothers being chased by PairOoboo and his men.
Queen W	Oh good 'eavens. Sweet Mother of God. They're losing ground – they're losing ground!!!
Bugger	The whole army is following PairOoboo! The King is nowhere to be seen! O, Misfortune Dire! Help! Hellllppppppp!!!
Queen W	Ooops, there goes Taggerlarse. My royal son – struck down by flying balls!!
Bugger	Alas! Yet see, bold Ruggerlarse now makes a stand! Go Ruggerlarse!
Queen W	Oh dear – surrounded.
Bugger	Oops – looks like he's copped it. Captain Crappering just sliced him in two like you would a big old sausage.
Queen W	Alas and alack, the rebels – they are pentrating our defenses. They are mounting the stairs, forsooth!
	[THE CLAMOUR GROWS.]

18

Queen W & Buggerlarse	*[ON THEIR KNEES.]* God defend us!
Bugger	For sure – 'tis Ooboo – bring it on, thou bastard!

scenefourthesame

the doors are kicked in, daddyoo-oo-oo and the mob bust through them.

Père Ubu	Buggelarse! Yeah? Wellcomeonthenan davaggohmyson – iffyouthinkyerardenuff!!!
Bugger	As God is my shield, I shall defend my Mother to the death. Let he who first gives way be corpsèd. En Guarde!!!!
Père Ubu	Crappering – take over. I'mouttahere.
A Pro-Ubu Soldier	*[STEPPING IN.]* Buggerlarse – have at thee!
Bugger	Take that, fuckface! *[HE SPLITS THE SOLDIER'S NODDLE OPEN.]*
Queen W	Oh I say Buggerlarse, well played!
	[SEVERAL MORE SOLDIERS, STICKING THEIR OAR IN.] Oh Buggerlarse, we're coming to getcha!
	[BUGGER FLAILS AROUND WITH HIS BLADE LIKE HE WAS A WINDMILL, AND SLICES UP THE LOT.]
Bugger	Hooligans! Pissartists! Republicans!
Père Ubu	Fuckit, I'm getting stuck in anyway –
Bugger	Mother – use thy hidden passage!

19

Queen W	But my son, my son, how shallst thou escape?
Bugger	I'll follow soonest.
Père Ubu	Somebody nab that queen! Fuck, she got away. And as for you, fuckface –
Bugger	Mine is the right, sayeth the Lord... *[HE SLASHES UBU'S SAUSAGE WITH A TERRIBLE BLOW.]* Mother – I'm right behind you!
	[PRINCE BUGGELARSE DISAPPEARS UP THE QUEEN'S SECRET PASSAGE.]

actwoscenefive
a cavern up some snowy mountain
young buggerlarse enters with the fair rosamonder aka queen wenceslarse following.

Bugger	We'll be quite safe here.
Queen W	I do hope so dear *[SHE COLLAPSES ON THE SNOW.]* Oh Buggerlarse – I can no further tread!
Bugger	Mummy – what's wrong?
Queen W	I fear I am not well, my son, and may not live the hour.
Bugger	Are you feeling chilly, Mamma?
Queen W	The sides of nature cannot thus long sustain it!!! The king dead – our family dispersèd all – and thou – thou, my son! The very noblest of our race... forced to traipse these mountains like a common brigand.

Bugger	Ya and just look who's doing the bloody forcing! This bloody Pear Ooboo no less – born in the gutter, dragged up god knows bloody where... there's a bloody shyster and ne're-do-well, if you *don't* mind. And to think that Papa made him a Cunt only yesterday. Not that that bloody stopped him committing bloody assault and battery on Papa. Forsooth.
Queen W	Oh, Buggerlarse my son! When I recall to the sessions of sweet silent thought how happy and glorious we all were pre-Ubu... but now, alas, what has come all over us!!!
Bugger	Chin up, Ma, best foot forward – and I'm still next in line, remember.
Queen W	'Tis my greatest wish to see you next enthroned dear boy – but never shall I greet that happy dawn.
Bugger	Oh, get it together Ma – but wait; she pales – she falls – O, helphelphelp, helphelp! Yet answer came there none. Her heart – oh no – 'tis stilled! Dead! Dead! How can this be! O, Ubu foul, thou claim'st another soul!!! *[HE BURIES HIS FACE IN HIS HANDS AND SOBS.]* Sweet Christ – what burdens must a Crowned Prince bear! Orphaned – fourteen – and Vengeance now my task! *[HE FALLS DEEP IN PRAYER AND THEN INTO DEEP DESPAIR. MEANWHILE, THE GHOSTS OF GOOD KING WENCESLARSE, HIS OTHER TWO SONS AND THE FAIR ROSAMONDER AKA QUEEN W., SURROUNDED BY ALL THEIR ROYAL ANCESTORS, APPEAR IN THE*

21

CAVE. THERE ARE SO MANY ANCESTORS THAT THE CAVE IS STANDING ROOM ONLY. THE OLDEST ROYAL ANCESTOR APPROACHES THE PROSTRATE BUGGERLARSE AND GENTLY ROUSES HIM FROM SLEEP] What's this I see? My family – my royal ancestors – what ghostly miracle is this?

The Shade Know, Young Buggerlarse, that I in life was one Matthias of Konisberg, the Founder of this Royal Line. I give thee here an instrument of Vengeance. *[HE GIVES HIM A BLOODY GREAT SWORD.]* God grant thy blade sleep not till Th'Ooboobastard's bloody blood doth stain its point – and thy royal line's restor'd. Remember meeeeeee...

The Shades Remember usssss...

[THE SHADES VANISH, LEAVING BUGGERLARSE IN A POSTURE OF SOLITARY ECSTASY.]

acttwoscenesix
le palais royale; ubu enthroned.
père ubu, mère ubu, captain crappering.

Père Ubu I won't, I won't, I won't. Why should I give *that* bunch of losers any money?

Capt. Crap Sire, the voters expect any regime change to be celebrated with a few giveaways...

Mère Ubu Get busy with the burgers and handouts, sunshine, or you'll be out on your arse by teatime.

22

Père Ubu	Burgers, OK; handouts, never. Look, somebody go and get three old nags out the royal stables, and then find me the mincing machine. The proles won't know the difference.
Mère Ubu	O hark at this one. Who made you posh all of a sudden?
Père Ubu	I'll say it again, I'm only doin' this for the money. Not a fucking fifty p piece – alright?
Mère Ubu	And this is the man who's just got his hands on the Crown Jewels of Poloneyland.
Capt. Crap	Look, I know; the palace chapel, that's absolutely stuffed with treasures – how about we distribute some of them?
Père Ubu	Listen fuckface, you touch a fucking thing –
Capt. Crap	But Ubudad, if you don't give the people some handouts, they won't pay their taxes.
Père Ubu	Fuck. Seriously?
Mère Ubu	Duh.
Père Ubu	Oh, all right then... three million quid – in cash – and five hundred cows, medium rare. But I gets one of the burgerz.

[THEY EXIT.]

acttwosceneseven

the courtyard of the palace, filled with a capacity crowd.

ubudad (crowned), mère ubu, capt. crappering, humble serving-drudges bearing platters of burgers, the people of poland.

The People	Hooray! God Save the King! God Save Our Gracious Ubu, Long Live our Noble Ubu, God Save the Ubu, etc.
Père Ubu	*[CHUCKING GOLD AT THEM.]* Alright alright, calm down, plenty for everybody. Loyal Subjects, it gives one not one iota of pleasure to be chucking away dosh like this, but your Royal Mummy UbuMum tell's me that's how it works. And now you have to pay me lots of taxes, right?
The People	Yeah fine whatever no problem yeah.
Capt. Crap	Blimey Ubumum, look at 'em fighting over the dosh. I predict a riot.
Mère Ubu	No fuckin' manners. Oh my lordy look at that one, someone's totally bashed her head in.
Père Ubu	What a fuckin' circus eh... better bring me some more boxes of dosh.
Capt. Crap	I say, how about making them compete for it?
Père Ubu	Brilliant! *[TO THE PEOPLE.]* Friends, Romans, Cunts; see these 'ere boxes; whatsinnem? Three hundred million smackers in solid gold coins, that's what, and each and ev'ry one of 'em personaly orfenticated by yer actual Royal Mintymint of this ere Poloneyland. Now; who wants

24

some? Right; thought so. Well 'ere's the rules. All competitors, line up down the bottom of the courtyard there; when I wave my hanky, off you go, and whoever wins gets the lot. And... waitforitforit – all the runners-up, there's this other box, right, just 'ere – and you all get sumphing outta that one. No fuckin' losers in *this* country, right?

The People   Oh yeah! Ubooo-oooo-oooo-oooH!
You never got nuffink like this with that old Wencelarse, didya?

Père Ubu   *[TO MÈRE UBU, WITH JOY.]* Hear that, Mummy? They fuckin' love me.

[ALL THE PEOPLE LINE UP DOWN THE BOTTOM OF THE COURTARD.]

Père Ubu   Onyamarx! Ready –

The People   We're ready, Daddy!!!!

Père Ubu   Steady –

The People   Steady yeah yeah!!!

Père Ubu   Goooooooh!!!!

[THE RACE BEGINS WITH EVERYBODY JOSTLING. CHAOS AND TOTAL FUCKIN' NOISE.]

Capt. Crap   And they're coming up on the inside now...

Père Ubu   ... Ooops there goes the front-runner –

Mère Ubu   – No, he's back on 'is feet...

Capt. Crap   Oh no! Pipped at the post – it's the other guy what won it –

[THE ONE WHO WAS COMING SECOND WINS THE RACE.]

The People   Long Live Michael Fedorovitch!
Long Live Michael Fedorovitch!

Michael Fedorovitch   Majesty, how can I possibly thank you –

Père Ubu   Don't mention it mate. Off you pop with your winnings. And everyone else, get stuck in divvying up this lot. And play nice, alright?

The People   Long Live Michael Fedorovitch! Long live King UbuDaddy!

Père Ubu   And I tell you what, friends; all back to ours!! I declare this... the People's Palace – and officially invite the whole fuckin' lottofya round for burger din-dins.

The People   Ooboo-oo-oo-oo-ooh! He's the best the King ever!!

[THE PEOPLE ALL PILE INTO THE PALACE. WE HEAR THE SOUNDS OF AN ORGY THAT CARRIES ON TILL DAWN.]

[THE CURTAIN FALLS.]

endofsecondact. it's all going splendidly.

actthreesceneone
the palais royale.
mummy and daddy ubu (crowned), post-burger.

Père Ubu	Shitmesideways – WHOSE THE DADDY?? I've 'ad me dinner, I've bust me guts – now where's this 'ere royal cloakywoke I was promised?
Mère Ubu	'Angon, 'angon – we may be royal now Daddy, but we still gotta watch the pennies –
Père Ubu	Oh 'ark at 'er – Mrs Fuckin' Austerity all of sudden.
Mère Ubu	Coz it's all very naice *becoming* King, Daddy – buddow you gonna *stay* king? That is the question.
Père Ubu	You godda point there, Mummy.
Mère Ubu	I think that Duke of Lithuania's on our side...
Père Ubu	Oo?
Mère Ubu	Crappering – you made him a Duke, remember?
Père Ubu	Oh please, that loser. He wants to go polish turds quietly in a corner somewhere, or 'eel be losing iz Dukeship sharpish, I can tellyer.
Mère Ubu	I tellyer, DaddyU, that sort can turn very nasty...
Père Ubu	I'm not scared ovvim... and I'm not scared of Prancing Prince Buggerlarse neither.
Mère Ubu	Oh, think you've seen the last of that one, do you?

27

Père Ubu	Turdinggreattaxhikes, coarse I do. Wot's a king like me gotterfear from a fuckin' fourteenyearold.
Mère Ubu	Daddy, read my fuckin' lips. Spend a few quid; get the kid on your side.
Père Ubu	What, more fuckin' giveaways? Nononononono No!!! I've already spaffed twenty fuckin' million this morning.
Mère Ubu	You wanna watch your back, Daddy – that there princester'll 'ave you in the shit if you're not careful.
Père Ubu	Well at least you'll be right in there with me, Mother.
Mère Ubu	Will you fuckin' listen to what I'm sayin for once!! This Buggerlarse is gonna be a problem – he iz the legal heir, remember.
Père Ubu	Oh givvitarest! Legal, schmegal – you, is doin' my 'ead in, Mummy. Yeah – in fact – I'm gonna fuckin' smash you one – *[EXIT MUMMY UBU PURSUED BY A PÈRE.]*

actthreescenetwo
the throne room of the palais royale.
père ubu, mère ubu, soldiers (officers, privates), posh people (in chains), bankers, judges and solicitors.

Père Ubu	Bring me... the special BankBox wot is reserved for the receipt of Poshcash; also my PoshPeopleGrabbingHook – and my Posh Disposal Unit. Fank you. And now, bring me some Posh People.

[THE POSH PEOPLE ARE PUSHED TO THE FRONT BRUTALLY.]

Mère Ubu Oh go easy on them Daddy, there's a love...

Père Ubu I hereby decree that in order to make Us richer, all Posh people now get immediately deaded and their arsets seized.

The Posh Monstrous! I say! Don't just stand there officer do something!

Père Ubu First Poshperson, approach the bench – and parse me the Grab'ook, would you. The ones what get condemned to deathness, I shove 'em through this trapdoor, see, like so – then they go through the Mighty Poshmincer, see – and end up in Posh Morgue – where they get their brains sucked out. *[TO THE FIRST POSHPERSON.]* And what's your name, fuckface?

First Posh I am the Cunt of Vitebsk.

Père Ubu Areyer. Andow much d'you earn a year?

First Posh About three million. In a good year. After taxes.

Père Ubu Guilty! *[HE GRABS HIM WITH THE GRABHOOK AND DROPS HIM THROUGH THE TRAP.]*

Mère Ubu Oh you ain't arf a terror, Daddy!!

Père Ubu Next! *[THE SECOND POSH DOES NOT REPLY.]* Cat gottyer tongue, richy?

Posh Two I, Sir, am the Duke of Poznan.

Père Ubu Are yer? Off you pop, then. Next! Fuck me you're looking rough mate.

Posh Three Duke Heartcastle; principal property holdings Riga, Tallin and Jelgeva.

29

Père Ubu	That all?
Posh Three	Er...
Père Ubu	Next!! *[DROPPING HIM DOWN THE CHUTE.]* And you are...?
Posh Four	Prince of Podolvia, Poldovia being a minor sub-Baltic principality –
Père Ubu	Yeah, yeah, yeah... Income?
Posh Four	Er, I was recently declared bankrupt.
Père Ubu	Not the sort of language we want to hear round 'ere thank you very much... Next! Name!!
Fifth Posh	I am the Lord Marshall of Thorn, Honorary Prince Palatine of the Polacks.
Père Ubu	Honorary, eh? So not paid nuffink?
Fifth Posh	I get by, your Majesty.
Père Ubu	Not past me you don't *[DOWN THE CHUTE.]* And what's your problem, Mother?
Mère Ubu	Well I do think you're being a touch bloodthirsty, dear.
Père Ubu	Right, and I'm also getting a touch fucking loaded. You wanna hear MY titles. Oi, you, Clerkface, read out the list of all the MY titles what are now in MY name now that that lot is officially deathed.
Clerk	Hear ye, hear ye, His Majesty Cunt of Sandomierz –
Père Ubu	Who are you calling a cunt – start with the big jobs first!!
Clerk	Er... His Majesty Prince of Podolalia; Archie-Duchy of Poshnan; Duchy of

	Heartcastle; Cunt of Sandomierz aforementioned; Even Greater Cunt of Vitebsk; Prince Palatine of the PollockBollocks, Lord Marshall of the Horn.
Père Ubu	Is that all?
Clerk	Totally.
Père Ubu	Totally my arse... OK, hear ye, hear ye, since I am totally not rich enough yet, I hereby announce the deadment of all remaining Poshers, and the assumption by ME of all vacant titles and property holdings appertaining thereunto forsooth. *[THEY START TO PILE ALL THE REMAINING ARISTOCRACY DOWN THE SHUTE.]* Ohgeddafuckinmoveon!! – I wanna pass some laws, next. *[A FEW DISSENTING VOICES.]* Laws! We'll soon see about that...
Père Ubu	First of all, I'm gonna REFORM THE JUDICIARY... oh yeah... – then – wait for it...; I'm gonna do all the BANKERS. OK –
Some Judges	We must most strongly object –
Père Ubu	Oh shite the fuck up. Law One; in future, no Judges gets paid.
The Judges	But what will we live on!? We'll be poor!!
Père Ubu	No...; you keep all the fines off the people what you fine, and all the land off the people what you dead. Simples.
First Judge	Good Lord!
Second Judge	Scandalous!
Third Judge	Infamy! Infamy!

Fourth Judge	They've got it in for all of us, actually...
Tutti Judges	We refuse absolutely to serve as Judges under these conditions!!
Père Ubu	Oh get them down the chute, for fucks sake *[THEY RESIST IN VAIN.]*
Mère Ubu	But Daddy what happens now? Who will uphold the law and and assert proper control over the entire judicial system of this country?
Père Ubu	Guess who, baby. Gonna be great. Very great.
Mère Ubu	Are you sure that's legal?
Père Ubu	Watch me, cuntlips. And next on the agenda, like I say; Banking.
Bankers	There are absolutely no alterations to current financial regulations required.
Père Ubu	Think again, sweeties. As from today, fifty percent of all tax revenues goes straight to my personal account. Make Ubu great again. Oh yeah. Very great.
Banker	You cannot be serious.
Père Ubu	Gentlemen I hereby announce a new ten percent tax on all property, another one on all commerce and industry... and on all births marriages and deaths, oh yeah, fifteen quid a pop. Die and it costs ya!! Fuck and it costs ya!! Oh yeah! OOOBOOOO!!
First Banker	But that's insane –
Second Banker	It's bonkers –

Third Banker	Completely arse over tit!
Père Ubu	Yer know guys, you just TOTALLY fucked me off. All Bankers down the crapper! *[ALL THE BANKERS GET MINCED.]*
Mère Ubu	Well a fine old king you make Daddy – at this rate you'll soon'ave killed fuckin' evrybody –
Père Ubu	Oh shate up!!!
Mère Ubu	No more judges, no more Bankers –
Père Ubu	Don't you worry your pretty little head about it sweetheart, I can always go round collecting taxes myself... hey – idea!!!

actthreescenethree

a humble peasant dwelling somewhere on the outskirts of warsesore.

a few peasants assembled.

A Peasant	*[ENTERING.]* You'll never guess what's on the news. The King is dead, so are all the posh people, young Prince Buggerlarse has fled to the mountains with Fair Queen Rosamonder – and DaddyUbu's only gone and seized the throne of Poloneyland!
Another One	And that's not all. In Crack-Off's fair city, there saw I streets bestrewn with bodies of bankers and judges both, what the King himself had deaded – and now forsooth our taxes they are doubled – and 'tis spoken abroad that DaddyU comest here to collect them in fuckin' person!!!

Tutti	Gourd 'elp us! They say this Ooboodaddy's a real bloody bloodsucker – and that'is missus is even worse!
First Peasant	But hark; who knocks there on the door?
A Voice Off	Shitingsausagefuckfactories – open up, crapstuffers; taxes, cracksies – show me the fuckin' MONEY!
	[THE DOOR GIVES WAY AND IN CRASHES UBU WITH A PACK OF CASH-GRABBERS.]

actthreescenefour

Père Ubu	Right, ooze the oldest? *[AN OLD PEASANT STEPS FORWARD.]* Washer name?
The Peasant	Stanislarse Leczinski.
Père Ubu	Ok, shitster, listen up, or this lot get mediaeval on your ass. Oi, are you lissnin?
Stanislarse	But Sire yoove not said nuffin!
Père Ubu	I HAVE BEEN MAKING A SPEECHY SPEECH FOR AT LEAST THE LAST ROYAL FUCKIN' HOUR, FUCKFACE!! However, think I've come all the way out here just to listen to the sound of my own voice, dooya?
Stanislarse	The thought never crorst my mind.
Père Ubu	Good; now; what I'm ackcherly here for is to let you lot know that I wanna see your taxlolly, pronto, on pain of immmediate fuckin' deadness. And now, my little Cash-

34

	hounds, if you would be so good as to wheel on the Cashcart. *[THE CASH-HOUNDS WHEEL ON THE CART.]*
Stanislarse	But Sire, we pay no more taxes than One Hundred and Fifty Two Smackers per annum – and we've paid this year already – on April 5th – six weeks ago – just like the form said –
Père Ubu	I'm sure you have, matey, BUT, I've changed the system, see, and under this new system, everyone asda pay their taxes twice, plus any extras what I thinks up later. That way, I get rich quick, I kill lotsa people and then I fuckoffowdervit. Simples.
Peasantry	Oh Mr Ubu, have pity kind sir. We are but humble low-paid careworkers!!
Père Ubu	Like I fuckin' care! Cough.
Peasantry	But we can't – we've paid already.
Père Ubu	Cough, or I'll ave your guts not only for garters but wrapped right round my fucking cock, alright? And, shitestirrers, I am your fucking king!!!
Peasantry	Oh no you isn't! Up the workers! God Save Prince Buggerlarse, Once and Rightful King of Poloneyland!!
Père Ubu	Times up! My ministers of finance; do your worst.
	[A FIGHT ENSUES; THE GAFF GETS SMASHED UP; STANISLARSE ALONE ESCAPES AND SETS OUT ACROSS THE PLAIN. UBU STAYS PUT TO HOOVER UP THE CASH...]

actthreescenefive

a dingeon in dunce-inane castle; captain crappering, strung up in chains; père ubu.

Père Ubu	Captain Crappering – hooze a fuckin' Duke now, eh? Look don't get sore matey, it's just the way the cookie crumbles. You wanted me to pay back a few quid what I owed you; I didn't fancy it; you come over all counter-Ubu conspiracy like – and now, you's strung up in a dingeon. Buggermebankways, mister – you gotta say I'm doing a good job on this King malarkey.
Capt. Crap	Watch thy back, o Ubu!! Bare five days yet thou hast been King, and steeped so far in murder, the saints themselves do weep!! The blood of Wenceslarse and all his nobles pleads loud to Heaven for Vengeance!
Père Ubu	Blimey mate, I 'ope your cock's as big as your dictionary. Were you to escape, I'm sure things could all turn very nasty – how ever, so far as I'm aware, these dingeons of Castle Dunce-Inance have never yet let slip a guest, so... sleep tight, hope the rats don't bite – and if they do – watch yer bollocks.

[HE GOES. THE GAOLERS COME AND LOCK ALL THE LOCKS.]

36

actthreescenesix

five days later
the palais of the tsar, moscow.

tsar alexis (and his court); captain crappering.

Tsar Alex	Yet sure, Captain Crappering, was't not thou, O ignoblest of mercenaries, that didst facilitate the treasonous deadening of our royal cousin Wenceslarse?
Capt. Crap	Tsar-Sire, I humbly crave your pardon. It was DaddyOoboo wot made me done it.
Tsar Alex	Oh you is such a fibber! Well, what ist thou wants?
Capt. Crap	Well, thing is, the OobooDadster had me locked up for conspiracy, right, but then I escaped, right, whatever, and now I've galloped five days and nights across the Russian Steppes to beg your Imperial pardon. Ok?
Tsar Alex	Wotcher gonna give me to show you really mean it?
Capt. Crap	My loyal sword – and this floorplan of Ooboo's Castle DunceInane.
Tsar Alex	I'll happily take your sword, handsome – but please, not the floorplan. I don't want anyone saying I cheat, militarily.
Capt. Crap	They say one of Wenceslarse's sons still lives – Young Buggerlarse. To see him on the throne, Sire, I'd lay down my life!
Tsar Alex	Would you? Hmmnn. What rank didst thou hold in the Polonial army?

37

Capt. Crap	Commander of the Fifth Royal Drag-goons of Vilnius, Sire, then I worked for Daddy Ooboo – then I was Duke of Lithuania. For a bit.
Tsar Alex	OK, well, I hereby name thee Sub-Lieutenant of my Tenth Russki Cossacks, and don't you fuckin' forget it. Do well out there, sunshine – and you won't be sorry.
Capt. Crap	Yowsa! Courage lackst I not, Sire.
Tsar Alex	That'll do! Depart our presence.
	[HE DOES.]

actthreesceneseven
ubu's security-council meeting room back in poland.
père ubu, mère ubu, a motley crew of finance regulators.

Père Ubu	I declare this meeting open, so everybody listen up and stay calm. First we're gonna talk finances, then, second item, I wanna discuss this little plan I have for me regulating the weather personally. Making it rain. Oh yeah.
A Financier	Very good, Ooboodaddy.
Mère Ubu	What a shitbrain.
Père Ubu	Hey, Mrs ShitLady, less of the foulmouth, OK? Now, I gotta tell you guys, the economy is really doing a great job. Really a great big one. Prostitooshun – booming.

	Burnt-out buildings – we got 'em pretty much everywhere. We got people on their knees, trying to meet their basic living needs – so all good. Really great. Really big greatgood.
A Financier	And the new taxes, how are they going down?
Mère Ubu	They's going down shite. The marriage-tax; thirty seven pee, so far. And that's with Daddy personally taking people up the aisle.
Père Ubu	Oi, Mrs FuckingFinancialFuckuppery Fuckface; read my ears; I mean lobes; I mean watch my arse – aaargh, fuckit, you've made me fuck up now! You always wanna make me look like I'm fucking stupid... I mean fuck my hairy arsehole, missus, I – *[A MESSENGER ENTERS.]* Whadderyouwant? Fuckoffowdervit, fuckface, or I'm gonna shove your shit so far up your fuckin' arse you won't take a crap till Shitmas! *[EXIT THE MESSENGER.]*
Mère Ubu	Ooh, look,'es left a letter...
Père Ubu	You read it. You've got me pretty fuckindiscumwankulated here. Also, I can't read. But I bet it's from that Crappering, right?
Mère Ubu	Right... And 'e sez the Czar of Russkia and 'im got on like a 'ouse on fire, so he's gonna invade you, put Buggerlarse back on the throne, and then he's going to kill you personally.
Père Ubu	I done wanna die! Mummmmmeeeee!!! –

the big bad man's coming to kill me!!!
JesusMaryJoseph, I'm a good boy I am – I'll
give back all the money – promise –
look, look, I'm lighting ya candles!! I'm
holding a fuckin' Bible yeah? O – O – what
shall become of me!!!

*[HE BREAKS DOWN AND STARTS
SOBBING HIS GUTS OUT.]*

Mère Ubu	Daddy, there's only one way outta here.
Père Ubu	Speak to me, baby.
Mère Ubu	*[CHANNELLING GLENN CLOSE IN "DANGEROUS LIASONS".]* Waaaaaaarrrr!!!!
Everyone	O yeah! Yeah! Warwarwarwarwar! Waaaaaaaaaaaaaarrrrr!!!!
Père Ubu	Do I still get killed?
Financier I	Immediate issue of call-up papers –
Financier II	Mobilise All Reserve Units –
Financier III	Bigger guns, bigger bangs, bigger Russia-buggers –
Financier IV	Increased Fucking Military Spending!!!
Père Ubu	Oioioioioi'ang on, 'ang on... Spending? I wanna kill people, not pay'em... Sod that for a game of soldiers! First you want me to go to war, then you tell me it's gonna cost me money? Shitteringfuckinshitfucks guys, look, you go to war if you want to – I'm not spending a fucking penny.
Financiers	Waaaaaaaaaaaaaaaaaaaaarrrrrrrrrrrr!!!! War! War! War! War!

40

actthreesceneeight
king ubu kits up for combat.
the camp outside warsesore.

Soldier Johnnies	God Save UbuKing! God Save Poloney land!
Père Ubu	Mother, pass me my breastplate and my bashingstick. Fuck me itseavy – I'm never gonna be able to run away when I need to in this lot...
Mère Ubu	Cowardy custard...
Père Ubu	Look Mother, my shitstabber won't sheathe – and this banking bloody armourjobby doesn't banking bloody fit me – and those Ruskies are coming to get me!
A Soldier Johnny	Sire Ubu, thy gaskins exposeth thy gonads!!
Père Ubu	Sonny, I'm gonna cunt your bollocks off and bank them right up your bandersnatch innerfuckinminnit!!
Mère Ubu	Honestly look at the state of 'im – all tin hat and no trousers. 'E looks like a fuckin' armour-plated aubergine.
Père Ubu	I shall now mount. Bring forth the royal horse, the nag yclept "LollySteed".
Mère Ubu	Oh, Daddy I don't think poor old Lollysteed'll stand the weight. 'E's eaten nuffink these last five days – in fact I 'ear 'e's practically dead already.
Père Ubu	'Ang on – I've been paying you twelve bob housekeeping a day to keep that nasty old

41

nag in wild oats – and now you tell me he can't take the weight? Either you're fucking lyin' to me, Mother, or you've been snitching the oats-money. *[MÈRE UBU BLUSHES AND FLUTTERS HER EYELIDS IN SHAME.]* Fuckit; bring me the Lollysteed – 'cause I ain't walking, I'll tell you that for nuffin'.

[THEY BRING ON A REALLY, REALLY HUGE HORSE; LOLLYSTEED.]

Right, OK, let's get mounting. Oops. Nearly. Fuck. *[THE HORSE MOVES.]* Somebody stop this Arse moving about willyer, I could fucking coppit if I fall off wearing this lot...

Mère Ubu   What a wanker. Oh – 'e's up.
No, 'e's off again...

Père Ubu   Is there a doctor in the arse – I'm practickly fuckin' dying 'ere... Right. Fuck There we go. Off to war and kill fuckin' evrybody. Line up, you lot. Anyone gets out of step and I'll rip your teeth out and shove your eyesockets right up your fucking arseholes, alright?

Mère Ubu   Good luck, dear.

Père Ubu   By the way missus, I'm appointing you Regent for the duration. However, I am taking the Royal Cashbooks with me, so fuckin' wotchit, alright, 'cause I'll know if you nick anything else? And I'm also leaving my trusty Lieutenant Musclefuck here to keep an eye on you. Adieu, Mother.

Mère Ubu   Go kill yourself a Czar, bigboy.

Père Ubu   Sure thing baby. I'm gonna fuck him so far
up the fuckshute his cunt is going to meet
his neck on the way back down.
Dy'aknowhaddamean?

*[THE ARMY MOVES OUT TO THE
SOUND OF FANFARE.]*

Mère Ubu   *[ALONE.]* Right. Now fartface is safely out
the way, down to bisness; one, bump off
Buggerlarse – two; get me 'ands on the
royal treasure.

[HERE ENDETH ACT THE THIRD.]

actfoursceneone
the crypt of warsesore cathedral, an ancient resting-place of the royal house of poloneyland.

Mère Ubu   Where's this 'ere treasure then? I can't find
no secret compartment nowhere... I've
counted thirteen gravestones along from
the tomb of Ladislarse the Well-Hung, like
they said I had to... but somebody's been
'avin' a larf methinks... Wadeaminnit!
This one sounds 'ollow... put yer back into
it, Mother, it's only a sodding tombstone...
not budgin', eh?... time to deploy this 'ere
trusty old Ubuhook, methinks. There
yago!! Ooooh... gold – gold I tell you!!
... plus a few royal skellingtons. Right;
where's me 'andbag?... and the rest...
But 'ark, what noise is this? Do these old
graves yet crypt some living soul?...
Nah – you're imaginin' it, Mother...
Right... any more for any more – for sure,
fair argent-stuff deserves the light of day, not
to lie in some mouldy tombland... That
noise again! My presence here doth me the
willies give – I'll stick the stone back, come
back for the rest tomorrer –

A Voice,   Never, Mummy U! Never – never – never...
emanating
from the
Sepulchre of
Sigsmond the
Unready

> *[MÈRE UBU GRABS HER LOOT AND*
> *SCRAMBLES OUT OF THE CRYPT BY*
> *MEANS OF A CONCEALED BACK PASSAGE.]*

actfourscenetwo

the main square in warsesore.

prince buggerlarse and his insurgents; soldiers; members of the proletariat.

Bugger	Once more into the breach, dear friends – cry God for Poloneyland and King Wenceslarse. Daddy Ubu has fled the town – that old Pretender – which leaves only the foul witch UberMum and her protector Musclefuckbetween us and my rightful throne. Proud I shall be to march thus at your head!
Tutti	Buggerlarse! Buggerlarse-arse-arse-arse-arse!!!
Bugger	And – wait for it – to abolish forthwith all Ubutaxes!!
Tutti	Arse-arse-arse-arse-arse!!! To the Palais Royale, lads! Death to the traitors!
Bugger	But see – see where comes Mamma Oob– attended – uponst yon battlements!
Mère Ubu	So whaddayoulot want – aaaaargh! 'Tis Buggerlarse!!
	[THE PROLETARIAT CHUCK ROCKS AT MÈRE UBU AND HER GUARDS.]
1ˢᵗ Mèreguard	Oh do be careful, you'll smash the winders!
2ⁿᵈ Mèreguard	By St George, I do believe I'm a gonner...
3ʳᵈ Mèreguard	Fuck me sideways, that's me done...
4ᵗʰ Mèreguard	Kiss me, Hardy –
Bugger	I say, keep chucking, lads!!
Lt. Muscle	Come on then sunshine – ifyoufinkyou'refuckingardenuff!!!

45

*[HE WHIPS OUT HIS MIGHTY
BLADE AND PROCEEDS TO WREAK
HAVOC ON A PREDICTABLY MASSIVE
SCALE.]*

Bugger   OK, OK, OK... Oi! Muscle! You and me,
matey – alright?

[THEY FIGHT 121.]

Lt. Muscle   Aaaargh – I die, I die – I die!!

Bugger   Victory, my friends! Now, where's Mother!

*[THE SUDDEN BRAYING OF TRUMPETS!
THE REMNANTS OF THE POLISH
ARISTOCRACY HAS COME TO JOIN THE
FIGHT AGAINST MÈRE UBU'S VILE
DICTATORSHIP.]*

Bugger   Strewtth, it's the cavalry! – Come,
gentlemen, onwards – and let's bring
the old witch to justice!

Tutti   String her up! String her up! String her up!

*[MÈRE UBU GETS AWAY – PURSUED
BY THE WHOLE POPULATION OF
POLONEYLAND. LOTS OF GUNFIRE,
STONES FLYING THROUGH THE AIR,
ETC, ETC.]*

actfourscenethree

meanwhile, the polish army is marching through ukraine. lollysteed is on his last legs and being dragged along.

Père Ubu　　God-Damn, God-Dick, God-Sausage –
we're doomed for sure, so tired and thirsty
be we all. Come, Soldier – lug you now my
Cashhelmet – and you, Sir Corporal, take
thus my Shitter-snackers and my Pokey
Pokestick – for they are heavy too by far,
and I must rest my weary arse.

*[THE SOLDIER-JOHNNIES DO WHAT
HE SAYS.]*

**Private
Prompt**　　Uh... bit weird the Russkies aren't showed
up, what?

Père Ubu　　God Rot our cashflow, that permitst not
transport fitting to our state... to save
our foundering nags, by foot thus slog we
many a weary mile... Were'st I in Poland
now – with physics labs and scientists
a-plenty – for sure I would invent some
car'o'th'air, to waft us hence at speed...

CPL Cordon　　Behold – why, 'tis Nicolarse Nackleby –
and approaching apace.

Père Ubu　　What news dost bring, that makes his
breath all pants?

Nackleby　　Sire, sire – all is lost! The Polish are
revolting – Musclefuck slain –
BigMammaUbu fled to the mountains.

Père Ubu　　Bird of ill-omen, screech-owl of doom,
ill-counted chicken of bad news – why

47

roost'st thou thus with me? And who hast done all this, forsooth – Prancing Prince Buggerlarse? Yeah, right, that piece of underage fuckup. Whence comst thou, soldier?

Nackleby From Warsesore, great king – where Bugglearsyan banners flout the sky, and fan our people cold –

Père Ubu Son, if I believed you, you, me and the army'd be heading there right now. However, you clearly have shit for brains, and that is totally fakefuck news. Check out the intel, soldier; the Russians will be here any minute. And your DaddyU is standing by right here and now to give'em cash and awe up the goddam crapshute.

General Flunk Reporting for duty, DaddyU; Russkies at three o'clock, sah!

Père Ubu So they are, soldier. Now you're talkin. If only there were some way out of here... but we're stuck on this hill, and looks like we're gonna be sitting fucks, godammit!

Soldier Johnnies Russkies! The Russkies are coming!!

Père Ubu OK, Gennlemen; listen up. We're gonna hold the high ground here – not much dumb-ass point in descending to their level, right... and your Noble Leader here is going stay right in the middle *here* while you all rally right round him. OK? Great. And I'm gonna recommend that you'all load up those rifles just as full of lead as you can get'em, boys – 'cause evry fuckin' bullet, that's one more fuckin' Russkie deaded yes

48

sir and no longer tryin to get up my ass, right!!! I'm gonna put the er Infantiles down here at the bottom of the hill here... you guys get to rough those Russkies up a little and get the killin' started... then we're gonna whack'em with the Mountin' Cavalry boys *here*... then kick'em when they're down with a little heavy Artillery fired from this here windmill *here*. And I'm gonna be right here *in* the fuckin' windmill, see, firin' out this here windmill winder with my good ole cashpistol – lettin' them have it where the sun don't shine with my pokeypoker – yessir!! – fuck with me, fellas, and you're gonna feel it right up your Russian ass!

Officers   Siryessir!

Père Ubu   Follow the plan; stick with the man. What hour ist now, Gen'ral?

Flunk   Eleven of the morning, sah!

Père Ubu   Ok then; time for lunch. Those Russkies never fight before twelve. General, tell the troops; take a break – take a crap – and meanwhile – let's all sing the CashSpangled Banner like we fuckin' mean it!

[FLUNK EXITS. THE ARMY SINGS:]

The Army   **Oh say can you see, Papa Ubu and God! They're So Fullershiiiit – but deliver the Money!**

Père Ubu   Oh you guys, you crack me up –

[A RUSSKIE CANNONBALL DISPRUPTS THE PROCEEDINGS BY BREAKING A SAIL OFF THE WINDMILL WITH A DIRECT STRIKE.]

49

Père Ubu   Oh no – please don't hurt me – God, this is
Ubu – donthurtmedownhurmee – wait –
OK – they missed me. Phew!

actfourscenefour

A Captain   Sah, sah! Russkies gaining ground, sah!

Père Ubu   And waddyawannme to fuckin' do about it?
I didn'tstart it... Ohforfuckssakeyeahbut
nobutyeahbutnobutyeahbutOK.
Gentlemen; once more into the belch.

Flunk   Cannonball coming in!

    [IT LANDS. BOOM! ETC.]

Père Ubu   Fuck this – way too many balls flying about
– like this could seriously endanger Your
Noble Leader, guys. Everybody Else,
Chaaaaaaaarge!!!!

    *[EVERYBODY HEADS DOWN ONTO
THE PLAIN AND THE TWO ARMIES
ENGAGE. THE LOWER SLOPES OF THE
HILL ARE OBSCURED BY CLOUDS OF
SMOKE...]*

A Russian   *[SMITING.]* For Bogh Ih Chzar!!

Nackleby   Dead – dead – and never called me Mother!

Père Ubu   You're gonna be sorry you did that, you –
you – Russiafucker!!! – with your
sneakysnarky Russiafuck bullet-bungler –
that I bet shoots blanks – yeah – YEAH?

    *[THE RUSSIAN FIRES A REVOLVER AT
UBU.]*

Père Ubu   Aaaargh! Owwwww!!! He shot me!!! I'm

fuckin' leaking here guys!!! Holes! Blood! Funeral! Tombstone... *[PLAYS DEAD; THE RUSSKIE FALLS FOR HIS RUSE.]* Oh dear, p'r'aps not. *[GRABS HIM SNEAKILY.]* Now I've gotcha... Yeah? Yeah? *[RIPS HIM OPEN.]* Now who's larfin, eh? Wanna start something do ya?

Flunk   One more push lads, those Russkies are on the run!

Père Ubu   Speaking of runs, where's the crapper...

Russian Troops   Hoorar! Hoorar! I'Chzar!! I'Chzar!!!!

*[THE TSAR APPEARS –
ACCOMPANIED BY TREACHEROUS
CAPTAIN CRAPPERING, IN DISGUISE.]*

A Polognese Sodjer   Sire! Fall back! 'Tis the Tsar!!!

A Second Sodjer   Blimey! We can't 'old 'em much longer!!

A Third Sodjer   Aaaargh! That's four brave lads topped just by that big bugger next to him!!

Capt. Crap   Fancy summa this, do ya! Take that, Pole-arse!!! They don't like it up'em!!

[HE MASSACRES LOTS OF POLES.]

Père Ubu   Onward, lads! Let's get the bastard! Fuck a Russkie! Up the Ubu!! That's the way to do it!!!

His Troops   Yay! Nailthefucker!!

Capt. Crap   By Saint George, I am o'ercome...

Père Ubu   *[RECOGNISING HIM.]* Whhhaaaatt? Captain Crappering! Dear Loyal Friend,

51

forsooth, my army and I are right glad
to seeya! And now... I am so going to slice
ya! Bring me the Royal Snickersnacks!
[A BANG.] Ah! Oh! They got me! Wiv a
cannonball! Arefarver, whatartinevvun,
hollowed be thy name, I'm a good boy I am
– yeah, yeah, that was definitely a cannon
ball what hit me –

Capt. Crap	More like a fuckin' water-pistol –
Père Ubu	Takin the piss, are we? Take that! *[HE TEARS INTO HIM.]*
Flunk	Sire, we advance on all sides.
Père Ubu	I see we do – but knackered I am forsooth, what with all this 'ere army malarkey. For gods sake let us sit upon the ground and have a drink. Where's my hipflask, soldier?
Flunk	Sure, Sire, yon Czar might have one you could nick?
Père Ubu	Thou speakst aright. Shitstick – to thy work – and Cashbonce, be not backward in coming forward. May our royal Pokey-Woker now slay, slice and slaughter this Emprah of the Russias to fuckin' bits. To arms! My horse – my horse – for fucksake where's my 'orse? *[HE MOUNTS UP AND CHARGES AT THE CZAR.]*
A Czarist Bodyguard	Wotch out, Majesty!!
Père Ubu	Shuddit! Ah! Ow! Leave it out, mate – no, stop muckin' abaht – it wasn't me what done it, honest –

	[HE GETS AWAY, BUT THE CZAR PURSUES HIM.]
Père Ubu	Hairy Mary, he doesn't fuckin' give up, does he? What did I ever do to him? Oh Lordy, who put that ditch there? Ditches to the left of me, Russkies to the right – here I am, stuck in the fuckin' – oh well, ere goes – aaaaargh!!!
	[HE CLOSES HIS EYES AND – STILL ON HIS HORSE – LEAPS THE DITCH. THE CZAR, IN PURSUIT, DROPS RIGHT IN IT.]
The Czar	Oh, great, stuck in a bloody ditch...
The Poles	Na na na na-na, stuck in a di-itch...
	[THE POLES BEAT UP ON THE CZAR.]
Père Ubu	OK... eye-opening, ready or not *[HE OPENS HIS EYES AGAIN.]* Ooo – somebody's in trouble... And gawblimey those Polish boys are giving him a good bashing... Givvim one from me lads... Oh I can 'ardly bear to watch, they is bein so vilent. And – obvs – this was all part of the plan. Oh yeah. Big plan. Very big. The pokeystick was totally in full working order, and absolutely I would have taken this guy down... apart from a few courage issues which we have had going on, obviously – and obviously there were responsibility issues here, questions of you know military er dignity, yeah, dignity stuff, right, big dignity issues here, especially protecting the er legs, right, the er legs of the horse here, the Cashnag, very big issue,

very big, very very big... and our Cashnag is the best, it is the biggest, it is the most resilient... but obviously, sometimes in Life, there are ditches, right? And this was very big ditch, very very big ditch – and can I tell you? Who fell in it? Right? So who is now totally in Cashcontrol? Totally. Oh Yeah. Oobooyeah. Oo-oo-oo.

OK guys so I'm making a speech here.

Guys?

OK... so let's er... er...

[THE RUSSKIES RALLY AND RESCUE THE CZAR.]

Flunk	I'm afraid they are rather gaining the upper hand Sire. In fact, complete omnishamble, what?
Père Ubu	OK; so clearly, right now, we fall back. Or in. Up. Go Poland!! Right?
The Polish Army	Let's get outta here!!

[THE RUSSKIES TURN THE TIDE.]

Père Ubu Fuck, I gotta get outta here too. We got people, we got army, we got bodies – I mean, like, we are totally not in a good situation here, right? *[SOMEBODY BUMPS INTO HIM.]* Hey!! Watch your feet, soldier – or you're gonna be feelin some of that UbuCashDaddyWarMachineAction up your ass, OK? I said OK, soldier? Phew. That was close. Ok... I'm outta here – and like quick, right, while Fuck Flunk over there is busy with the military whatever and can't see me...

54

[PÈRE UBU RUNS AWAY FROM THE BATTLE; AS HE SNEAKS OFF, WE SEE THE CZAR AND HIS RUSSKIES ROUTING THE POLISH ARMY.]

actfourscenefive

a cave in lithuania. it snows.

père ubu, corporal crashbang and private wallop.

Père Ubu	So, like, what's with the weather, Corporal Crashbang? Your CashDad is freezin his fuckin' balls off 'ere.
Crashbang	Uh, hey, like, OobooPop, what's with the running away thing? Like the terror thing, you know?
Père Ubu	I'm good with the terror just now thankyou soldier, but let's keep going with the running away, OK?
Wallop	*[UNDER HIS BREATH.]* Whadda piece of –
Père Ubu	How's it hanging, Private?
Wallop	Not so good, Boss. Situation Normal Totally Fucked Up. My gun just aint fuckin' firin' like it used to, Boss.
Père Ubu	Hang on in there soldier. That weapon's gonna be up and dealin' the deathload real soon, son. Look at your BossDaddy here – not a scratch on me, soldier, and I got at least four of those assholes where it hurts – and that's not counting the ones that were dead already when I shot 'em.
Wallop	Anyone huh know what happened to that little drummerboy I was fucking?

55

Crashbang	He copped it.
Père Ubu	Hey! In Flander's fields – no less – fair flowers also fell, 'fore that big old Reaper named Fate... Yet, Ladz, consol'st thou thuswise thy fainting, doubting selves; that young Drummerboy, fair poppy that he was, fell face to the foe, though sadly fucked owing to their superior very big numbers and firepower.
Crashbang and Wallop	Yeah. Fucked.
An Echo	Farked-ark ark ark ark hark!!!!
Wallop	What the? Guns out, boys.
Père Ubu	Oh gimme a fuckin' break, not more fucking Russians – Oi, you! one step closer and this pokeypoke goes right where the sun don't shine –

actfourscenesix
the same, plus a bear.

Wallop	Look beyindyer, Cashdaddy!
Père Ubu	Aw! It's a little lost doggy... here puppy puppy...
Crashbang	Daddy – that ain't no puppy, that's a fuckin' ginormous bear – just gimme a moment to get cocked and loaded here guys...
	[HE FUMBLES WITH HIS WEAPON.]
Père Ubu	A bear!! A bear!!!! Aaargh – done let him eat me – JesusJesusMary, I'm a gonner – it's cummin' for me – it's cummin' – it's cummin' – aaaaaaaaargh – oh; OK;

56

it's going for Corporal Crashbang. Great. Fuck me that was close.

[THE BEAR GOES FOR CRASHBANG; WALLOP DEFENDS HIM BY WHIPPING HIS BIG BLADE OUT AND GETTING STUCK IN. PÈRE UBU SCRAMBLES TO SAFETY UP ON A ROCK.]

Crashbang   Arrgh! Help me! Ubudaddy – heeeeeelllpp mmmmeeeee!!!!

Père Ubu   Calm down matey it's only a fuckin' bear. Everybody gets eaten sooner or later. I'm praying for ya – OK? *[HE PRAYS THROUGHOUT THE STRUGGLE BELOW.]* Our Fuckster, Which Farts in Havens, Hollow be Thy Name; Thy cash make me come, I will be Dumb, in Turd as it is in TaxHavens; Give us this way our dailycash, and forgive us our tax rises, as we tax those who vote against us, and lead us straight into deregulation, for thine is the cashflow, the power and the policeforce, Fuck Them.

Wallop   Hang on – I got this –

Crashbang   Get a fuckin' move on soldier, I'm getting fuckin' disembowelled here –

[PÈRE UBU PRAYS THROUGHOUT.]

Wallop   Come ere ya fucker...

Crashbang   He's got me! Jesus H Christ he's fuckin' got me!!!

Wallop   Take that, bearboy...

Crashbang   Oh yeah – yeah he's definitely bleeding now –

[THE BEAR SPOUTS BLOOD AND BELLOWS; PÈRE UBU CARRIES ON PRAYING; WALLOP GETS A GRENADE.]

57

Wallop	You keep hold of him, while I stick him with this here Bigbang Heavy Cummer –
Crashbang	I can't hold himmuch longer!!!
Wallop	*[FINALLY GETTING THE PIN OUT OF HIS GRENADE AND SHOVING IT UP THE BEAR'S ARSE.]*
	Goddit!!
	[THERE IS AN ALMIGHTY BANG AND THE BEAR FALLS DEAD. PÈRE UBU FINISHETH HIS PATERNOSTER.]
Père Ubu	... Fuck Them. OK, so is he deaded? Can I get down off my rock now?
Crashbang	*[CONTEMPTUOUSLY.]* Take your fuckin' time, daddy.
Père Ubu	*[CLIMBING DOWN.]* Yeah but yeah but OK but listen, OK, the fact that you are still alive right now – the fact that you are able to be still standing upright and shitting up this Lithuanian snow right now – that is, right, only on account of the great – really great – really great personal and selfless selfsacrifice of me, your Number One CashPrez, right, a Really Great Great Leader who has gone personally out on a limb here to keep right on praying for you in this emergency, right – who hath wielded the Sword of Prayer as righteously here as this brave soldier here has also been righteous with the contribution of his interpersonal explosive devices to this situation. Indeed I wanna tell you personally that so prayerfully and personally were we engaged right here in

	this situation, we even climbed a rock, oh yes, very big rock, very big, very very big, so we could get those prayers closer up and direct into Heaven, HeavenDirect yessir.
Crashbang	Crap.
Père Ubu	Whaddafuckinmonster, eh? Well, I guess I got us fixed for dinner here, troops. This here beardaddy sure is fat enough... reckon those Ancient Greeks could have used this one for their Trojan Horse his guts is so damned roomy... thank our lucky stars we aint seein those guts from the inside eh boys!
Crashbang	Uh-huh. And I sure as hell is hungry.
Wallop	I'm thinking bearburger.
Crashbang	Uh-yeah...
Père Ubu	Waitwaitwaitwait – you're gonna eat him raw? Aint we got nothing to light a fire with?
Wallop	We could uh blow off another grenade I guess.
Père Ubu	Great idea. Also, I saw a little forest back there a-ways, I bet there would be some dry twigs we could use for a fire, right? Hey Corporal, howzabout you go get us some twigs!

[CRASHBANG TRUDGES OFF INTO THE SHOW.] |
| **Wallop** | SirUbuSir, permission to butcher the bear, sir! |
| **Père Ubu** | Ok, Ok – but are you sure it's really dead? Look... you're pretty covered in blood already, soldier, so I'm gonna leave that to you. I'll er make us some fire while he's fetchin' us those there twigs. |

*[WALLOP STARTS BUTCHERING
THE BEAR.]*

Whoa – it moved!!

Wallop　Sir, this here bear is most definitely stiff and cold. Stiffstiffstiffie yessir!

Père Ubu　Well then we better get him cooked, soldier. Bear sure is better eatin' good and hot – and we gotta take care of the old CashPrez digestive tract, soldier.

Wallop　Like that ain't fulla shit already... *[OUT LOUD.]* You wanna lend a hand here SirUbuSir – or you just gonna watch?

Père Ubu　Oh I'm good. Watching. It is way tiring, being me, y'know?

Chrashbang Returning　Gettaloadathatsnow! Can't tell if it's the North Pole out there or New Fuckin' Jersey... And nightfall e.t.a. in one hour, I reckon – so let's get busy here, guys, while the light holds out.

Père Ubu　Hellyeah, guys – let's get that bear cooked for Crissake! Your Daddy's fuckin' starvin here!

Wallop　OK! That's it! Listen up, Mr Greedy President; you don't work – you don't eat.

Père Ubu　OK OK OK – it's only a fuckin' bear... you cut it up, I'll eat it raw. And while you're busy, I sure could do with a nap.

Wallop　Grrr...

Crashbang to Wallop　Private – leave it.

[UBU STARTS TO DOZE.]

All the more for us, right? He gets to chew on the bones after.

	[THE FIRE STARTS BURNING PROPERLY.]
Wallop	OK, now we're cooking.
Ubu	*[IN HIS SLEEP.]* Oh yeah warm me up baby. Aaargh, methinks I see Russkies. Will this night never end? Zzzzzzz...
	[UBU SLEEPS.]
Crashbang	Gee, I wish I knew if what they said on CNN was true – about MammaUbu being de-throned, I mean. You know, it just could be...
Wallop	Let's finish fixin' the fuckin' bear, OK?
Crashbang	But care'st thou not which way the wind doth blow? Knowing what ist – fake news or nay – that might be good, thinkst'ou not?
Wallop	To split with th'Ubudadster, or not to split – that is the question.
Crashbang	Let's sleep on't. Shit looks sometime clearer in the morning, forsooth.
Wallop	Yeah. Though 'tis easier to run in the dark.
Crashbang	Let's do it, soldier.
	[THEY SCARPER.]

actfoursceneseven
ubu talks in his sleep.

Père Ubu	Nyet, nyet... oh please mister russkie soldier sir – please don't stick it in me right out here, people might see. Hark – who knocks? ... Captain Crappering! What a shitstirrer –

61

one might almost think him a bear... Who
next – Aaargh! Out, out, damned
Buggerlarse! Infirm of purpose, give me the
pokeypoke. Who would have thought an
old bear would have had so much meat
on him! I didn't mean to do it, honest...
now, by the prick right up my bum, a
knocking still – oh yeahbutnobut –
the Czar!!! – please don't hit me,
Czarmeister!!! Who rises next, this last
and worst of spirits – 'Tis MommaU...!!!
But soft – who gave her all that gold?
Sure, wench, thou hast been rummaging
'mongst fair WarsesoreTown's encrypted
tombs, 'mongst the bones of Sigismondo
the MightyHung... Knock, knock – Yet
still 'tis Crappering! Out, out damned bear
I say – He hears not – he speaks not – for
sure, my loyal troops have whipped off his
nadgers... Nadgering, thefting, cropping the
cash-flow – 'tis a soldier's life. I'll drink to
that. Make Daddy Great Again. Daddy for
CashPrez. Cheers... cheerzzzzzzzzz...

[HE SLEEP. ACT FOUR FINITO.]

actfiveatfuckinglastactfivesceneone
it is night. the père ubu sleeps. the mère ubu
enters, without seeing him. total blackout.

Mère Ubu   At last somewhere to get out of this snow.
                 On me tod – still never mind – and what a
                 journey eh? Clean across Poloneyland in
                 just four days. And everyfink what could of
                 gone wrong – well let's just say it has.
                 Separated at last from Lardarse, I 'eaded
                 straight for that treasure-crypt and the lolly.
                 For my pains, I narrowly avoids getting
                 stoned by Buggerlarse and all that rabble.
                 Next, I loses my lovely Mr Musclefuck,
                 'im as was so gone on yer mother he
                 practically came every time 'ee looked at
                 me – and also, they tell me, even when
                 he didn't, which is a sure sign that it was
                 Lurve, Actually. 'Ee'd have let hisself be
                 chopped in two for me, that boy. And just to
                 prove it, he was. By that bastard
                 Buggerlarse; chip chop chip – hung – but
                 gawn and quartered... Honestly, I nearly
                 died. Then – well, I legged it, pursued by
                 an howling mob; got out the Paliss; made it
                 to the River Fistula – where all the bloody
                 bridges were only fuckin' closed already. So,
                 I am swam over, 'opin' to thus evade my
                 pursuers. Fat bloody chance. Whole bloody
                 place swarming with Tom Dick and
                 Aristocracy, every single one of 'em out to
                 fuckin' get me on account of all them taxes.
                 Whatever. Hemmed in, I was – hemmed,
                 by bloody great Poles. At last, I gives 'em
                 the slip – and then, would you mind,

63

there follows for your mother four fuckin'
days of fucking trudging across her own
fuckin' country in the drivin'fuckin'snow –
and now... 'ere we are. I 'aven't 'ad
a single thing to eat or drink in those hole
four days, would you mind – and that
fuckin' Buggerlarse is still snapping at my
heels I shouldn't wonder... still, reckon I'll
be safe in here. Gawd I'm cold and 'ungry.
Wish I knew what had happened to
Lardface... I mean my darlin'usband... And
to that Lollysteed of his. Starved to Death I
spect on account of somebody purloining
the Royal OatMoney... oh what a farkin
shame that was! Still, no use flogging a
dead orse. And you wanna know the
saddest bit of the hole farking story; the
treasure-money. I only 'ad to go and leave
it behind in farking Warsesore, didn't I. For
some fuckin' lucky chancer to pick up and
pocket I 'spect... fukkit...

Père Ubu *[SURFACING FROM SLEEP]* Grab 'er!
Somebody grab the Mamma! Grabber by
the pickers and stealers!!

Mère Ubu What the – Oh my gawd I don't believe it.
It's only DaddyOob, snorin is 'ead off right
fuckin' next to me. Ok, Ok; act normal.
Good morning, Roly Poly... sleep well did
you dear?

Père Ubu *[HAVING A NIGHTMARE.]* No – no no no,
Mr Bear – Exit Pursued By – This is the
chase... and I'm his fuckin' breakfast.
Sombody 'elp me!!!!

Mère Ubu What izzy fuckin' on about? Sounds like

	he's lorst it completely since I larst sore im. And who's he callin for elp from?
Père Ubu	Crashbang! Wallop! Where art thou! Daddy's scaaaaared... hangonhangon; somebody spoke. That's no fuckin' bear... Oi! Oooizzit? Where's me matches? Shate, must've dropped em on the battlefield...
Mère Ubu	*[ASIDE.]* OK Momma; work it. It's pitch black, 'ee carnt see a fing, so... make like you're an Supernatural Apparition, and scare 'im into forgiving your tresp-arses. Ooooo –
Père Ubu	Hairyfuckinmary... who goes there?
Mère Ubu	*[BOOMING.]* Ooooboooooo!! Dust to dust, arses to arses – I address thee now to pronounce thy Final Fate and Doom. Knowst thou not my voice? 'Tis The Gabriel Archangel, of the Final Trump, that speakest nought but Truth!
Père Ubu	Oh is that all, you had me worried there for a minute.
Mère Ubu	Silence, or my lips are sealed – and thy cock, it shall drop off!!
Père Ubu	Oh no please, not my cock, not my cock... sealed I shall stay, forsooth – pray you speak again, O Mrs Voice of Doom.
Mère Ubu	Ubu... thou art of all men... the fattest slob alive!
Père Ubu	Well you've got me there love, totally the fattest –
Mère Ubu	Silence, For FuckSake!! I mean God's!!!

Père Ubu	That's funny. I didn't know Archangels swore.
Mère Ubu	*[ASIDE.]* Shate. *[ALOUD.]* Art thou marrièd, O Ooboo?
Père Ubu	Totally. To Mrs Bitch From Hell.
Mère Ubu	Meanest thou sure Mrs Angel From Heaven.
Père Ubu	I meanest Mrs Total Fuckin' Nightmare, lady. That woman's got so much side you could cut yourself just fucking her.
Mère Ubu	You should try a little tenderness, Mr Ubu. Handled a little more naicely, she might prove a right little sex-bomb.
Père Ubu	Sexbum? Mother? Total fuckin' flat-arse.
Mère Ubu	You is not lissning, DaddyUbu; I pray you, wash out them lugholes. *[ASIDE.]* I'd better get a move on, 'tis almost morning... *[TO UBU.]* Ubu, some might say thy lady waife is an virtual Domestic Goddess –
Père Ubu	Some might say, she is an Neighbourhood Fuckin' Mattress –
Mère Ubu	No way she fucks around –
Père Ubu	Because no-one would touch her with a fuckin' large-pole –
Mère Ubu	She doesn't drink –
Père Ubu	Because I keep the booze under lock and key –
Mère Ubu	And she NEVER nicks nothing. Never.
Père Ubu	Oh really...
Mère Ubu	Never nicks a penny of her housekeeping money –
Père Ubu	Tell that to my fuckin' horse – never fed

	him for three months, she didn't, the poor bugger – died half way across the Ufuckinkraine.
Mère Ubu	Lies – the'ole lot of it. Your wife's a fucking saint... and you... you... you're a total miserable, cheapskating CUNT.
Père Ubu	And you, missus, is a total, fuckin', ARCHANGELIC FUDGEPACKER.
Mère Ubu	*[USING HER ANGEL-OF-DOOM-VOICE AGAIN.]* Oobooo – beware!!
Père Ubu	Oh, yeah, sorry, sorry, forgot who I was talking to for a minute there. Never meant a fucking word, alright? Your Archangelness.
Mère Ubu	Wast thou didst kill King Wencelarse, Ubu!!!!
Père Ubu	I didn't mean to, honest. It was Ma Ubu what made me do it.
Mère Ubu	AND didst dead his royal sons!!
Père Ubu	Well, yes... but only 'cause they wanted to dead me first, right?
Mère Ubu	Ooobooo, attend! There is but one way thou canst atone for these thy sins!
Père Ubu	Lay it down, baby. I've always wanted to be good, me. You know – like... a bishop, maybe. Pope. Saint. Our Ubu, which art tax haven –
Mère Ubu	To save thy dam-ned sole, thou must... forgive Mère Ubu for diddling the royal accounts. Ever so slightly.
Père Ubu	Oh I'll fuckin' forgive her alright – once I've smacked her all the way from 'ere to Christmas – and when she's brought my fucking horse back to life what she starved to fuckin' death!!!!

67

Mère Ubu	Oh you and your fucking horse already – but soft, what light through yonder cavemouth breaks? Alas, 'tis morningtime!
Père Ubu	Still, good to have confirmation that the missus IS a fuckin' thief. Good to have it on Divine Fuckin' Authority so to speak – and oh, what's this – Mrs Archangelic Apparition here has finally shut the fuck up. Has finally as you might say fucking stopped with the ArchAngelic Sarky-Sark Sarcasm. And good 'eavens, here comes the daylight... revealing no less than... Gawd Fuck Me Sideways With A Dead Fucking Horse – it's Mummy U!!!!
Mère Ubu	*[ACTING AFFRONTED.]* It is not! *[ARCH ANGELIC.]* I shalt excommunicate thee, Ooboooo!!
Père Ubu	Excommunicate my ARSE.
Mère Ubu	Blaspheme not, Cunty!
Père Ubu	Oh give it a rest missus. Look, I know it's you, so tell me; what on earth is you doin in the same cave as me?
Mère Ubu	Musclefuck died and them Poles is after me.
Père Ubu	Right. With me its Russkies. Looks like we're both up the same creek.
Mère Ubu	Right. And if I did have a paddle, I'd fuckin' brain ya with it!!
Père Ubu	Oh yeah? Time for you to meet my little fat friend here...
	[HE CHUCKS THE DEAD BEAR AT HER.]
Mère Ubu	*[COLLAPSING UNDER THE WEIGHT OF THE BEAR.]* Oh Gawd! Oh Lawd!

Geddimorf me! He's sittin on me... 'e's eating me...'es swallowing me... I'm bein' diiiiigessttttedddd!!!!

Père Ubu   Calm down dear, he's only a dead bear. Or – maybe not – no – *[MÈRE UBU WRESTLES UNDER THE BEAR SKIN.]* the beast lives – aaargh!! Quick – my rock *[PÈRE UBU SCRAMBLES BACK UP ON HIS ROCK.]* Our Farter, which arse tax haven, hollow be thy fame –

Mère Ubu   *[GETTING FREE...]* Now where's he gone?

Père Ubu   Oh good lord up she pops... No easy way of getting rid of you, is there?... Hangon – is that bear dead?

Mère Ubu   Course he is you fool – stiff as a fuckin' board. What's he doing in here anyway?

Père Ubu   *[CONFUSED.]* I don't know. Yes I do! He wanted to eat Smashgrab and Wallop, but I prayed him to death with a quick Our Father.

Mère Ubu   You ain't got no Father. I think you've lost a few fuckin' marbles in this 'ere war, Cashbonce.

Père Ubu   You're the one who's marbleshort, Cashwife.

Mère Ubu   Alright, alright... so tell me – how's it goin' for you anyway. The war.

Père Ubu   Well, to cut a long story short; despite my total fucking bravery... everybody keeps on hittin me!

Mère Ubu   What the Poles as well?

Père Ubu   You fuckin' betcha – and they's always shouting Up Buggerlarse, Up Wenceslarse.

Anyone'd think they blamed me for what's going down.

Mère Ubu   Buggerlarse deaded my lovely Sargent Musclefuck.

Père Ubu   So? He deaded half my farkin' army.

Mère Ubu   So?

Père Ubu   So – so – we're 'ere now, Rotface! And I'm Topdog!! *[HE PUNCHES HER AND PUSHES HER TO HER KNEES.]* Hit your knees and beg for mercy when I'm talking to ya, Missus!

Mère Ubu   Oh, Daddy –

Père Ubu   Oh Daddy Nuffink! Have you finished? Well I aint even fuckin' started. I'm gonna cut your nose off; I'm gonna pull yer air aht; I'm gonna poke my pokey-poker right up all available pokeholes – and then, I'm gonna remove your spine; I'm gonna go in through your arse – suck your fucking spine-marrow out bone by bone – take a bit of a detour to re-open ya fuckin' navel – and then – big finish – I'm gonna get John The Baptist all over your fuckin' neck, mis-sus – that's right, decapifuckingtation, actual Bible-stylee – New Testament, Old Testament – any way you slice it, missus, the neckbone aint gonna be connected to the head bone by the time this here Cashdaddy's finished with ya. How does that sound, Shitsausage?

                [HE RIPS HER.]

Mère Ubu   Oh Daddy, don't!

[THERE IS A GREAT BIG NOISE AT THE MOUTH OF THE CAVE.]

actfivescenetwo

buggerlarse and his troops swarm into the cave without seeing him.

Bugger	Once more into this cave, dear friends. Viva Poloneyland!
Père Ubu	Oldyerorses, Mister Poloneypersonwhozevveryooare – I woz just 'avin a private conversazione with my other arf ear, iff yew don't maind.
Bugger	*[STRIKING HIM.]* Have at thee, bumfuck – bigot – bellend – Belgian – Biden!!!
Père Ubu	*[HITTING BACK.]* Back atcha, paedo – pansy – pensioner – prick – Patel.
Mère Ubu	*[JOINING IN.]* Take that – chicken – chihuahua – chinkychonk Churchill choochoo –

[THE TROOPS HURL THEMSELVES ON THE OOBS, WHO FIGHT BACK WITH ALL THEIR MIGHT.] |
Père Ubu	Talk about reinforcements...
Mère Ubu	They've certainly got the staff...
Père Ubu	JesusHTurdingTurdpile, is there no fuckin' end?... And another one bites the dust...
Bugger	Keep at'em lads!!!
A Voice From Outside	Long Live DaddyOob, our Noble Cashleader!!

Père Ubu	At fuckin' last!! Here comes the cavalry. Get stuck in, Oobsters. Cashbash away!!
	[ENTER UBU'S SQUADDIES, LED BY CRASHBANG AND WALLOP. THEY HURL THEMSELVES INTO THE FRAY.]
Crashbang	Fuck a Polonester for Christmaaaaas!!
Wallop	Small world Daddy? We'll smack'em where it hurts – get you and the F.L.U. to the mouth of the cave – then you fuckin' run for it.
Père Ubu	You fuckin' betcha, soldier. Ow, that hurt!
Bugger	Lord – I am smited.
Stanislarse Leczinski	'Tis but a scratch, Sire, surely –
Bugger	Right – as you were – flesh wound only – Hold the line, men! Don't let the bastards get away!
Crashbang	Comin through!!! Makin' Ooboo Great Again Yessir!!!
Wallop	They sure don't like it up 'em, Daddyoob!!
Père Ubu	Oof – ah – oof – Ah, no, I've crapped my pants! Right – let's fuck the fuckin' fuck out of these fuckin' fucksters!! Ooboo-oo-oo – Ooboo – ooo-oooooo...
Crashbang	Two more to go, and we're outta here –
Père Ubu	*[KILLING THE LAST TWO POLONAISE BY BASHING THEM WITH THE DEAD BEAR.]* Anna one... anna two... *[HE GETS OUT OF THE CAVE.]* At fuckin' larst. OK; Everybody; on my count ruuuunnnnnn!!!!

actfivescenethree

the scene represents the republic of estonia, snowbound. the oobs and their troops are hotfooting it in retreat.

Père Ubu	Well, I think they've given up trying to catch us...
Mère Ubu	That Buggerlarse has gone off to get himself crowned, probably.
Père Ubu	Catch me wearing a fuckin' crown.
Mère Ubu	Absolutely, DaddyU.
	[THEY VANISH MIDST THE SNOWY WASTES.]

actfivescenefour

the bridge of a ship what is cruising along the baltic coastline. père ubu and his crew (mère, crashbang, wallop) are on that bridge.

The Captain	Quite a wind, what!
Père Ubu	'Tis true, sir Captain, that we do make our great escape on this your vessel with quite remarkable paciness. We have, as you might say, got a proper wind up.
Wallop	Yeah like right up my fuckin' ass...
	[A SUDDEN SQUALL BLOWS UP. THE SHIP FOUNDERS AMIDST BREAKERS.]
Père Ubu	Ooooh! Aaargh!! Gawwddd!! We're goin over! – I mean under!
The Captain	Splice the mainsail there! Reef the bosuns!!
Père Ubu	Ist wise, sir? Supposing the wind changeth

	direction – swiftly might we all be beneath the briny and promptly fish-lunch.
The Captain	Hold hard, me hearties. Steady as she blows.
Père Ubu	Never mind getting blown mate, whatever happened to land ahoy? I really wanna... you know... get somewhere... you know? Like, land. Ere, let me ave a go. OK. This is your captain speaking. Heave ho – about turn – now get your mizzens up your mainmast and your foc'sle down your foreskins, lads, cause we're going about. There we go. Luff in yer lanyards there... east by nor'east and hold your coarse, captain. *[THE WIND PICKS UP – THEY ALL FALL ABOUT.]*
The Captain	Run up the fore-rigs; lower the topsail. Yare! Yare! We split! We split!!!!
Père Ubu	Oh shuddit. Unfuck yer spinnaker, missus, and show us yer yardarm!!!
	[THEY DIE LAUGHING. A WAVE SWAMPS THE BOAT.]
Mère Ubu & Crashbang	We're riding along on the crest of wave...
	[ANOTHER HUGE WAVE.]
Wallop	*[SOAKED.]* Eternal father, strong to save, for fuck's sake stop these fuckin' waves...
Père Ubu	Oi – you – who do you have to fuck round here to get a drink?
	[THEY ALL BREAK OUT THE DRINK. THE SEA CALMS DOWN.]
Mère Ubu	Oh, think how lovely it would be be to see once again hoving into view one's

	dear old Poloneyland... all our old friends... the dear old house and home...
Père Ubu	Any day now, missus – any day.
Wallop	I tell yer, I'm so looking forward to dry land, I could shit.
The Captain	And won't we 'ave some tales to tell. When we get home. I should fucking coco.
Père Ubu	So should I. I fancy becoming Chancellor of the ExCheckArse. When we get home.
Mère Ubu	Oh I say, Daddy, won't that shake up the old place a bit!
Crashbang	What's this then? Fog? Fisher. Forties. North Sea... Germans Bite.
Wallop	Dogger. Humber. Thames Estewery.
Père Ubu	They calls it the Thems, on account of it belongs to Thems, not to Us.
Mère Ubu	You is so erudite, Daddy. Well I mist says it looks like a very naice cuntry. What do they call it?
Crashbang & Wallop	Engerland.
Mère Ubu	Nevererdovvit.
Père Ubu	Very nice... but there's no place like 'ome. is there.
Mère, Crashbang, Wallop	Oh no...
Père Ubu	Standstereason. I mean... if there weren't no place like home... there wouldn't be no people like us...
The Voice of the Fog	Land ahoy!!!!

FIN.